Naomi Jones   James Jones

ONE MORE TRY

OXFORD
UNIVERSITY PRESS

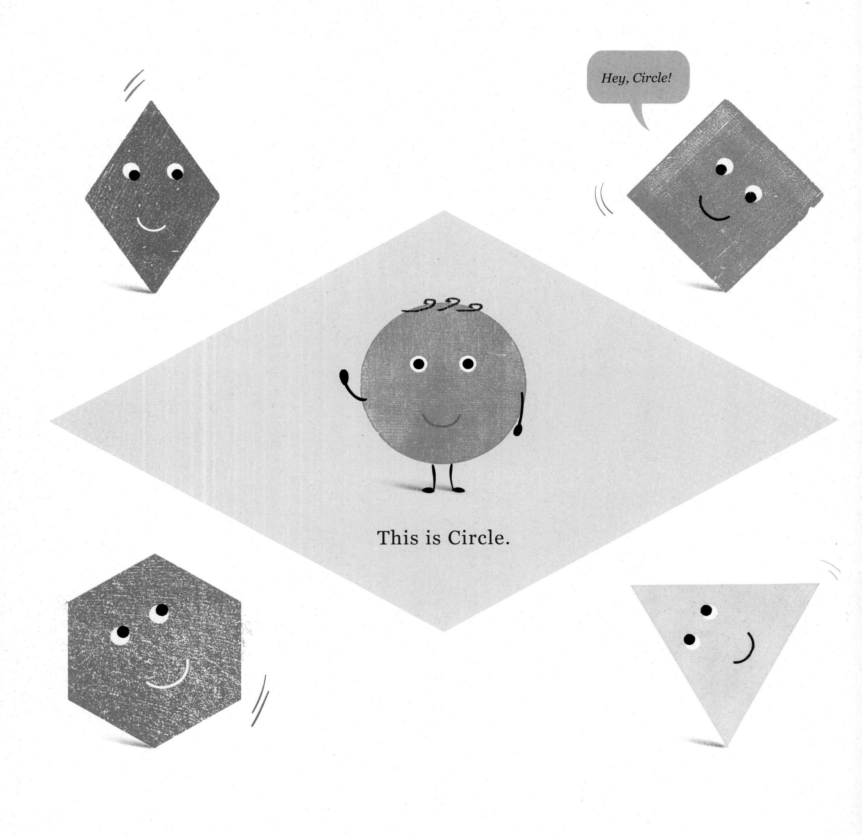

This is Circle.

To Janet and Paul,
for all their love.

OXFORD
UNIVERSITY PRESS

Great Clarendon Street, Oxford OX2 6DP

Oxford University Press is a department of the University of Oxford.
It furthers the University's objective of excellence in research, scholarship,
and education by publishing worldwide. Oxford is a registered trade mark of
Oxford University Press in the UK and in certain other countries

Text © Naomi Jones 2022

Illustrations © James Jones 2022

The moral rights of the author and artist have been asserted

Database right Oxford University Press (maker)

First published 2022

British Library Cataloguing in Publication Data available

ISBN: 978-0-19-277901-4

1 3 5 7 9 10 8 6 4 2

Printed in China

Paper used in the production of this book is a natural, recyclable product made
from wood grown in sustainable forests. The manufacturing process conforms
to the environmental regulations of the country of origin

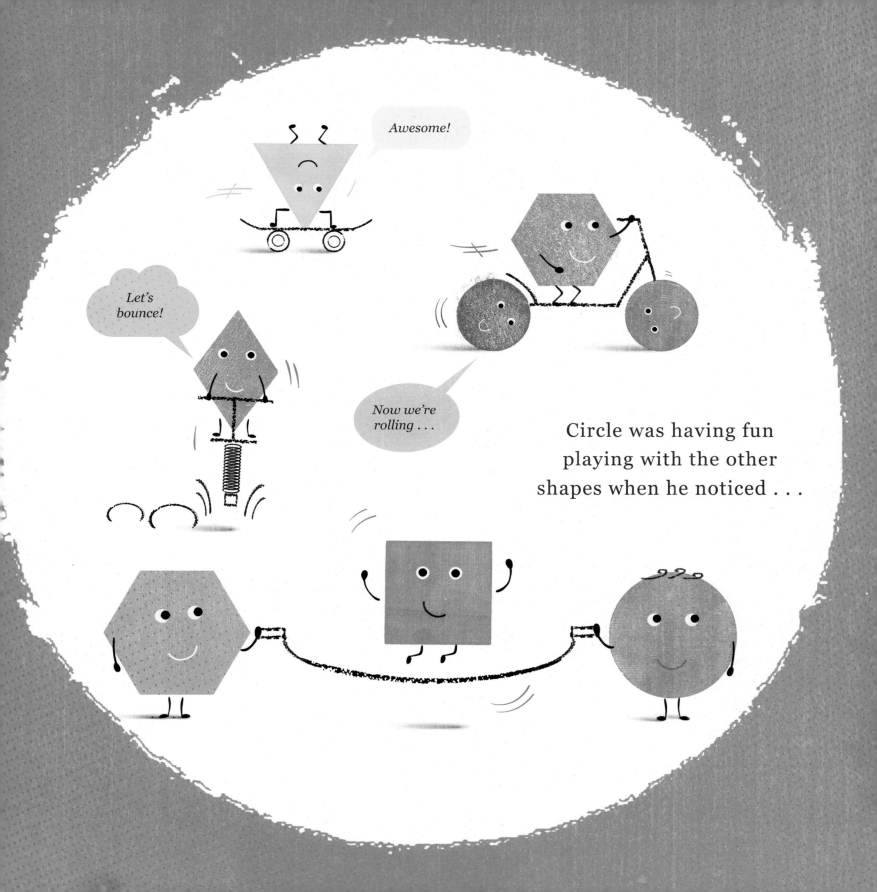

Circle was having fun
playing with the other
shapes when he noticed . . .

. . . the squares and hexagons
building a tower.

'That looks fun,'
said Circle. 'Shall we try
to build our own tower?'

It's just
so high . . .

. . . and so
perfect!

The shapes thought it was a great idea!

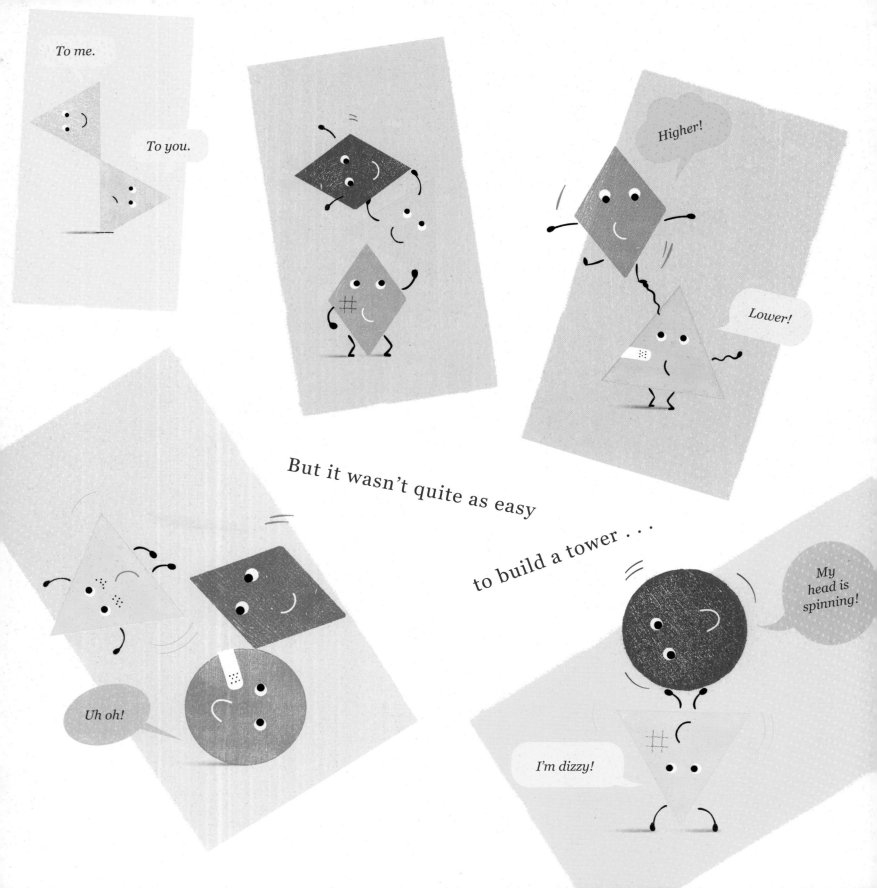

But it wasn't quite as easy

to build a tower . . .

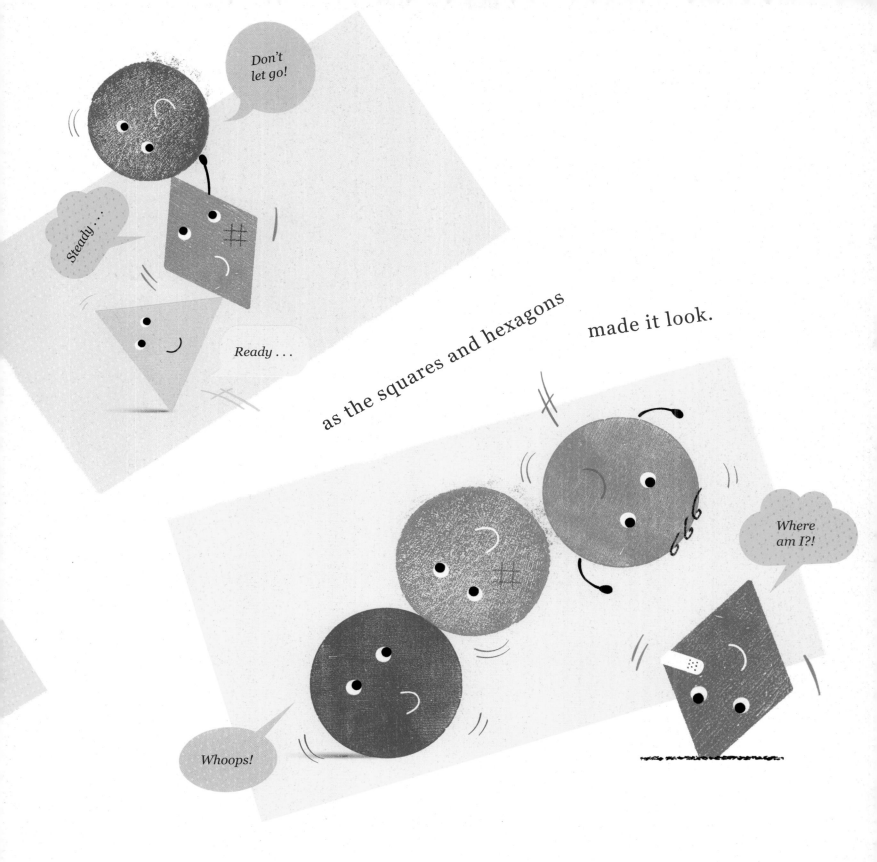

as the squares and hexagons made it look.

'There must be a way we
can do it,' Circle said.

'Maybe we just need
to be stronger?'

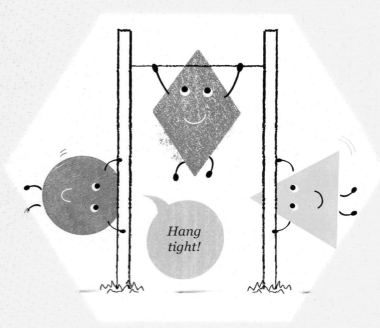

So the shapes did some workouts . . .

and

ran

some

races.

Being stronger
definitely helped . . .

Looking good!

but it didn't take long

before their tower

tumbled down again.

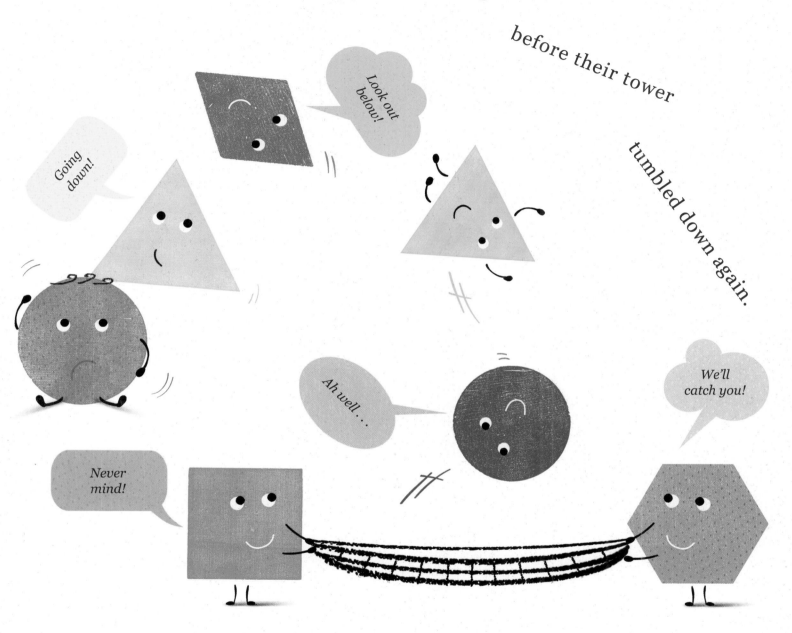

'Maybe only squares and hexagons
can build towers?' Circle wondered.

But he
wasn't ready
to give up.

'Perhaps we need
to be smarter?'
thought Circle.

So the shapes studied.

They used everything they'd learnt to help them build a tower.

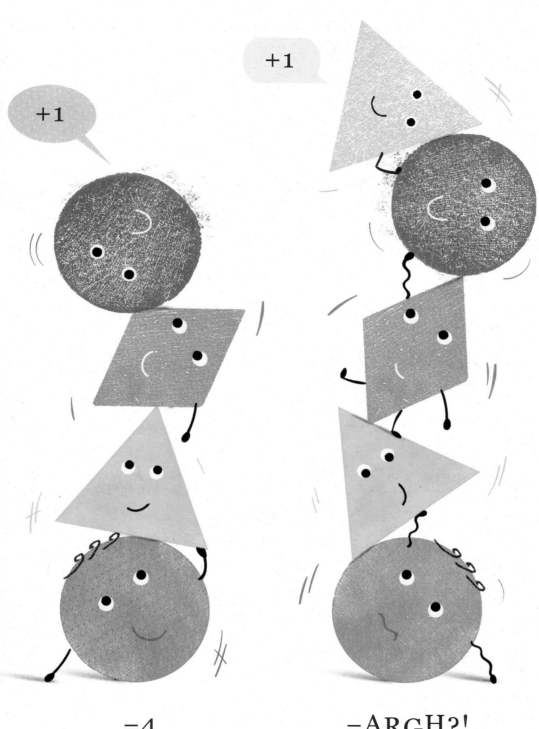

'It's definitely better,' Circle said, 'but it's still much wobblier than the one the squares and hexagons made.'

His friends all started
playing a new game, but
Circle was still determined
to build a better tower.

'Perhaps we need to look
at it from another angle,'
Triangle suggested.

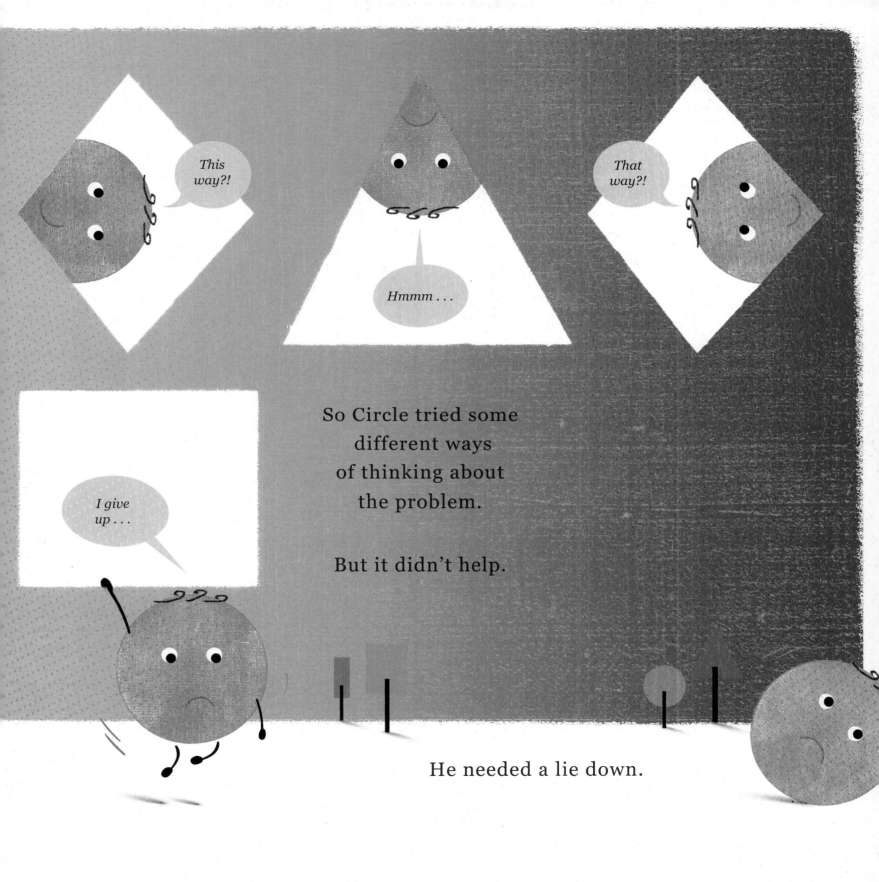

So Circle tried some
different ways
of thinking about
the problem.

But it didn't help.

He needed a lie down.

Circle looked up at the sky.

'Don't give up!' a star called down.

I just feel so flat.

'Keep trying and you'll find a way.'

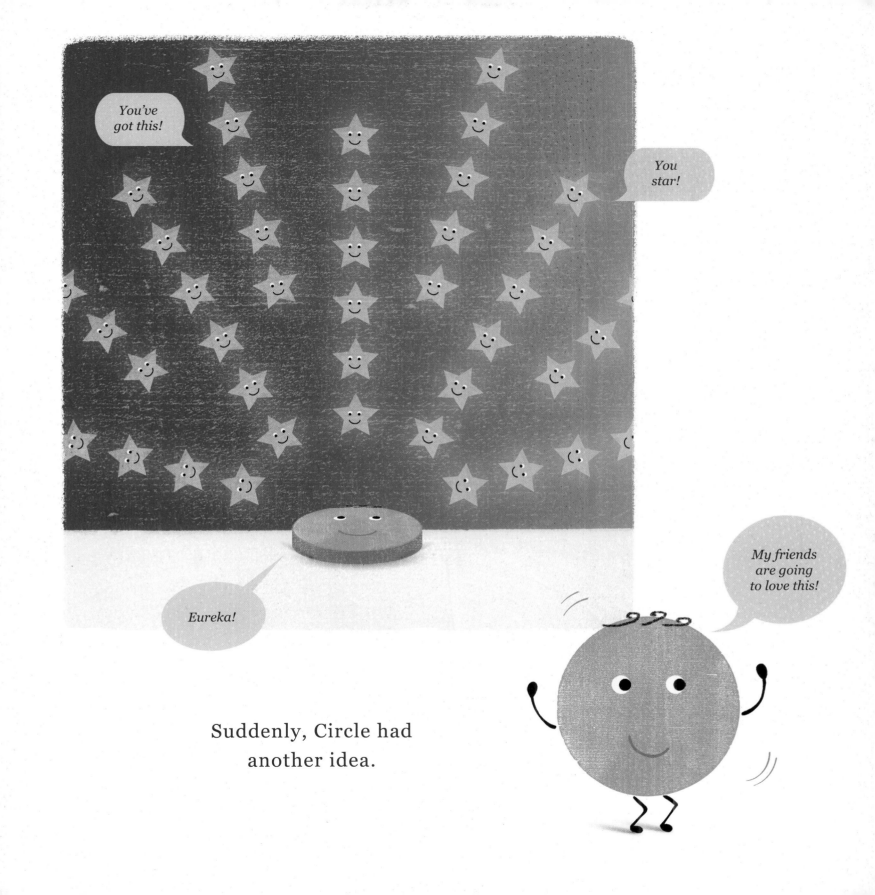

Suddenly, Circle had
another idea.

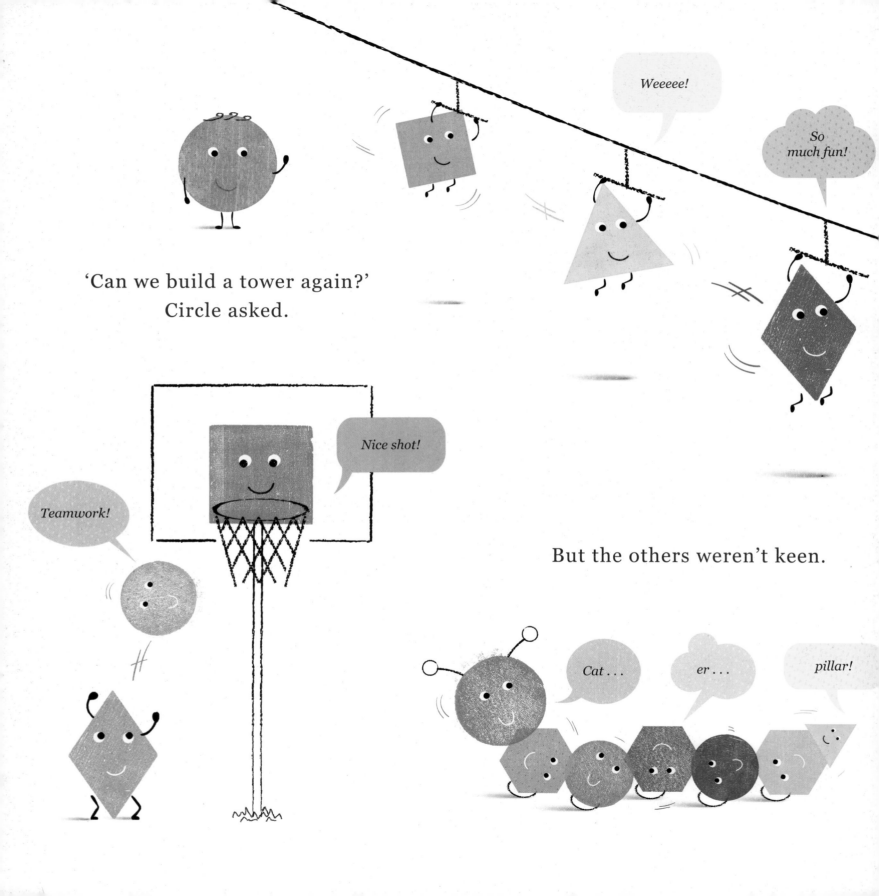

'Can we build a tower again?'
Circle asked.

But the others weren't keen.

'Please?' Circle said.
'Just one more try.'

So Circle showed everyone his plan.

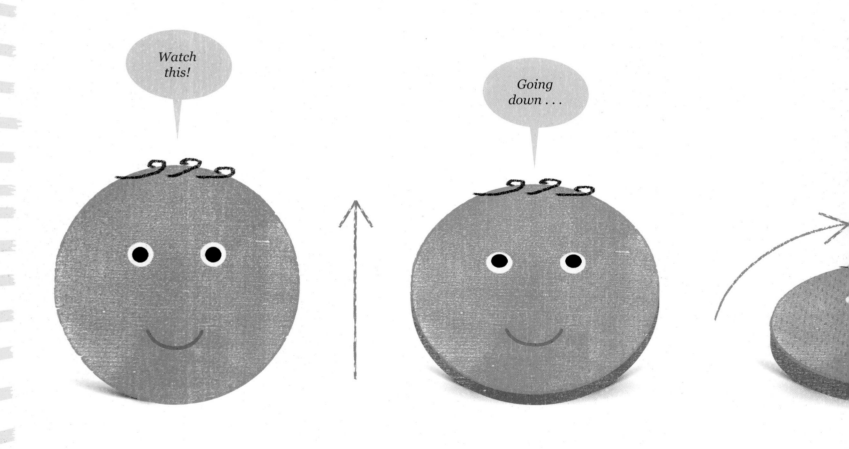

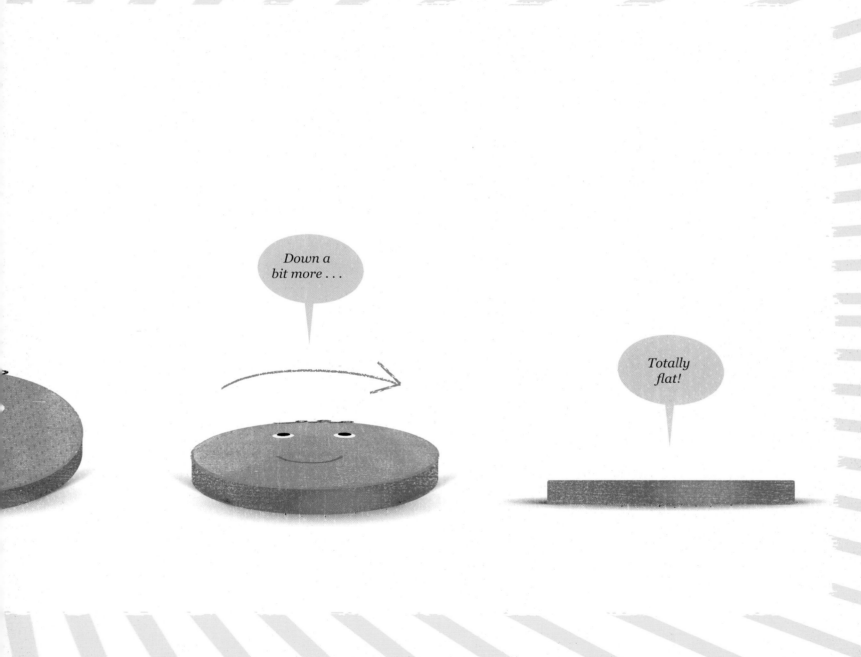

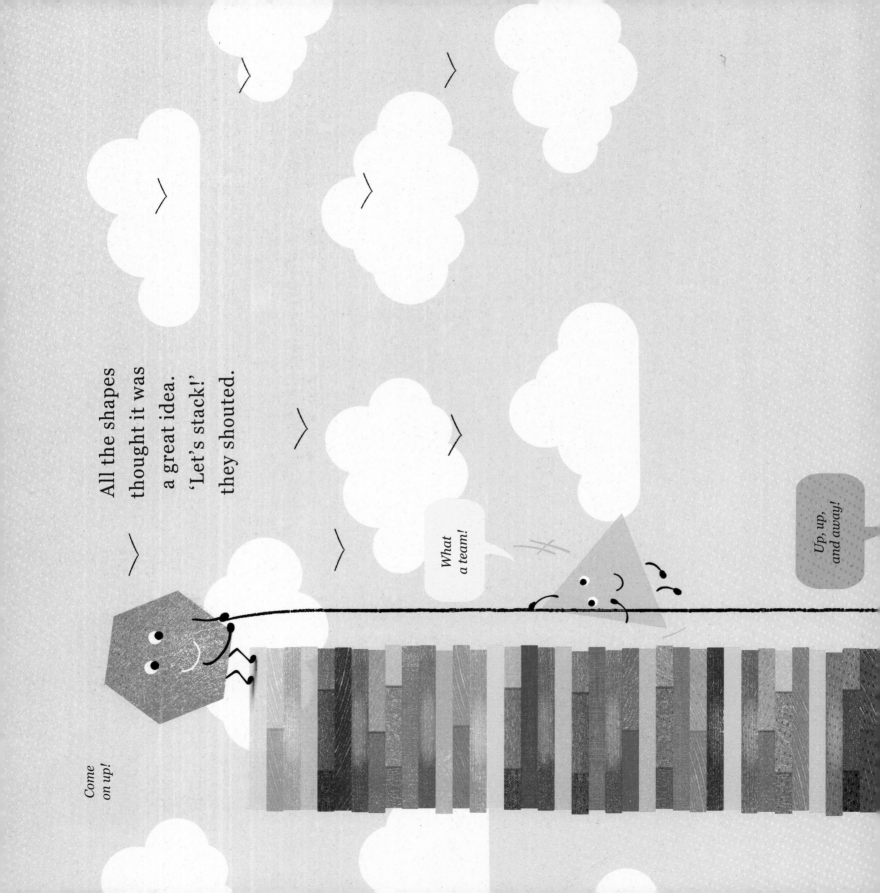

All the shapes thought it was a great idea. 'Let's stack!' they shouted.

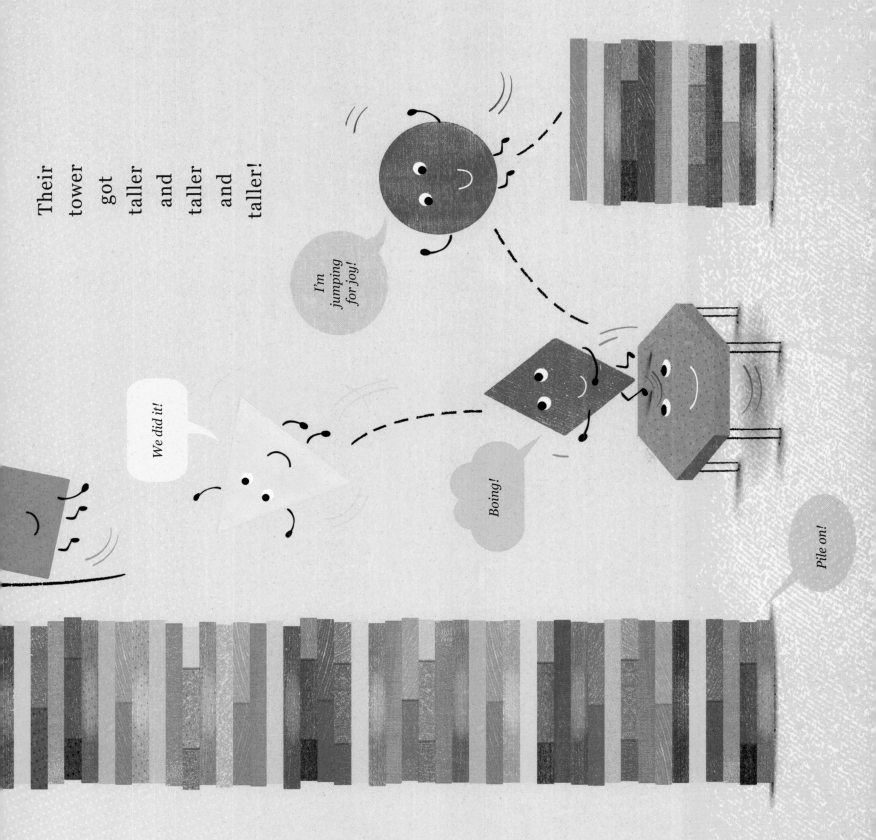

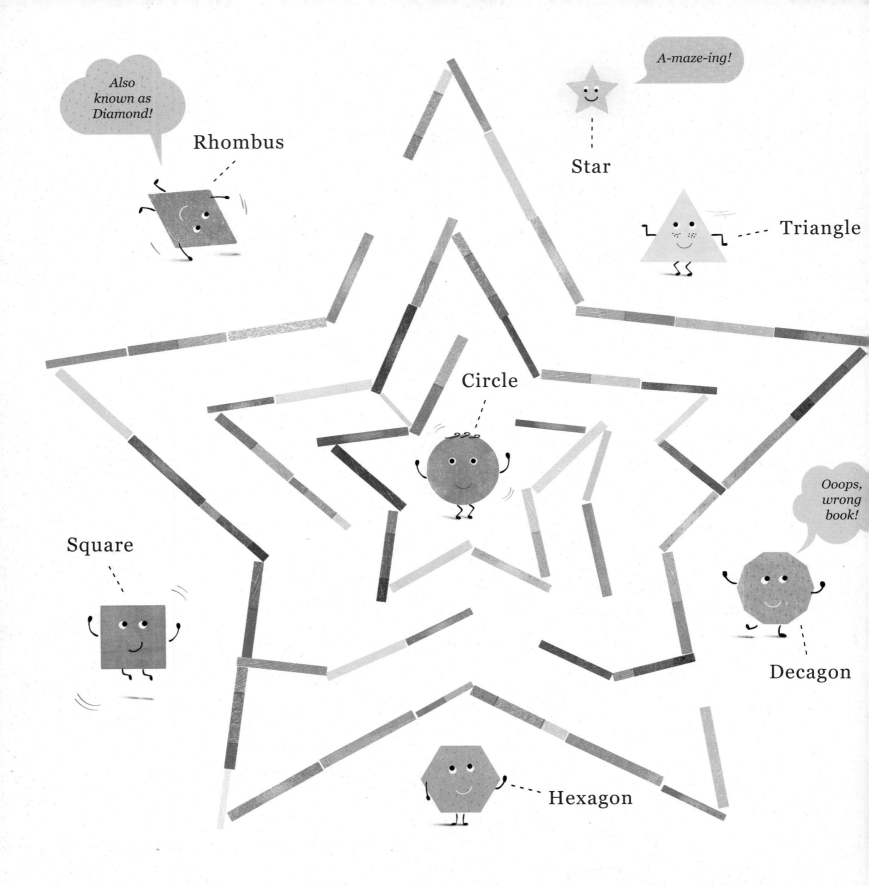